First World War
and Army of Occupation
War Diary
France, Belgium and Germany

52 DIVISION
Divisional Troops
Divisional Trench Mortar Batteries
1 May 1918 - 27 December 1918

WO95/2892/4

The Naval & Military Press Ltd
www.nmarchive.com
Published in association with The National Archives

Published by

The Naval & Military Press Ltd

Unit 10 Ridgewood Industrial Park,

Uckfield, East Sussex,

TN22 5QE England

Tel: +44 (0) 1825 749494

www.naval-military-press.com

www.nmarchive.com

This diary has been reprinted in facsimile from the original. Any imperfections are inevitably reproduced and the quality may fall short of modern type and cartographic standards.

© Crown Copyright
Images reproduced by permission of The National Archives, London, England, 2015.

Contents

Document type	Place/Title	Date From	Date To
Heading	WO95/2892/4 Divisional Trench Mortar Batteries		
Heading	52nd Division Trench Mortar Btys May-Dec 1918		
Heading	War Diary Of X 52 Trench Mortar Battery From 1.5.18 To 31.5.18		
War Diary	Valheureux	01/05/1918	11/05/1918
War Diary	Neuville St Vaast	12/05/1918	12/05/1918
War Diary	Vimy Sector	12/05/1918	31/05/1918
Heading	War Diary Of Y 52 Trench Mortar Batty From 1st May 1918 To 31st May 1918		
War Diary	Valheureux (near Doullens)	01/05/1918	07/05/1918
War Diary	Mont St Eloy	08/05/1918	08/05/1918
War Diary	Vimy Acheville Road	08/05/1918	08/05/1918
War Diary	Left Of Willerval	09/05/1918	09/05/1918
War Diary	Vimy Acheville Road	09/05/1918	14/05/1918
War Diary	Neuville St Vaast	10/05/1918	10/05/1918
War Diary	Vimy-Acheville Road	21/05/1918	28/05/1918
Miscellaneous	Headquarters, 52nd Division	06/07/1918	06/07/1918
War Diary	Neuville St Vaast	01/06/1918	07/06/1918
War Diary	Willerval	08/06/1918	28/06/1918
War Diary	Farbus Stn	29/06/1918	30/06/1918
War Diary	Neuville St. Vaast	01/06/1918	01/06/1918
War Diary	Vimy-Acheville Road	01/06/1918	04/06/1918
War Diary	Mont Foret Willerval Road	04/06/1918	04/06/1918
War Diary	Mont Foret Quarries	08/06/1918	08/06/1918
War Diary	Mont Foret Arleux Road	13/06/1918	13/06/1918
War Diary	Mont Foret Acheville Road	15/06/1918	17/06/1918
War Diary	Mont Foret Willerval Road	21/06/1918	21/06/1918
War Diary	Vimy	27/06/1918	27/06/1918
War Diary	Bois De La Chaudiere	28/06/1918	28/06/1918
Heading	War Diary 52nd Divisional Artillery Trench Mortars July 1st 1918 To July 31st 1918 Volume 1 Part VII		
War Diary	Neuville St Vaast	01/07/1918	31/07/1918
War Diary	Neuville St Vaast Vimy	01/07/1918	01/07/1918
War Diary	Vimy-Acheville Road	02/07/1918	02/07/1918
War Diary	Vimy	10/07/1918	21/07/1918
War Diary	Neuville St Vaast	22/07/1918	22/07/1918
War Diary	Ourton	22/07/1918	29/07/1918
War Diary	Bailleul	30/07/1918	30/07/1918
War Diary	Anzin	31/07/1918	31/07/1918
Heading	War Diary Of X/52 Trench Mortar Battery From 1st August 1918 To 31st August 1918 Vol 4		
War Diary	Anzin St Aubin Nth Of Scarpe	01/08/1918	01/08/1918
War Diary	Willerval Nth of Scarpe	02/08/1918	02/08/1918
War Diary	Willerval	04/08/1918	22/08/1918
War Diary	Anzin St Aubin	22/08/1918	22/08/1918
Heading	War Diary Of Y/52 Trench Mortar Battery From 1st August 1918 31st August 1918		
War Diary	Anzin St Aubin	01/08/1918	01/08/1918
War Diary	Bailleul	01/08/1918	17/08/1918
War Diary	River Scarpe W Of Fampoux	17/08/1918	17/08/1918

War Diary	Bailleul	18/08/1918	20/08/1918
War Diary	Anzin St Aubin	21/08/1918	23/08/1918
War Diary	River Scarpe W Of Fampoux	24/08/1918	27/08/1918
War Diary	Anzin St Aubin	27/08/1918	27/08/1918
Heading	War Diary Of Y/52 T.M Batty From 1st Sept 1918 To 30th Sept 1918 Vol 5		
War Diary	Anzin St Aubin	01/09/1918	01/09/1918
War Diary	Croisilles	11/09/1918	11/09/1918
War Diary	Queant	17/09/1918	19/09/1918
Heading	War Diary Of X/52 T.M. Batty From 1st Sept 1918 To 30th Sept 1918		
War Diary	Anzin St Aubin	01/09/1918	01/09/1918
War Diary	Croisilles	11/09/1918	11/09/1918
War Diary	Moeuvres	16/09/1918	30/09/1918
Heading	War Diary Of X/52nd T.M. Battery From 1st October 1918 To 31st October 1918		
War Diary	Noreuil	01/10/1918	03/10/1918
War Diary	Cantaing	04/10/1918	04/10/1918
War Diary	Moeuvres	05/10/1918	05/10/1918
War Diary	Cantaing	08/10/1918	10/10/1918
War Diary	Niergnies	11/10/1918	11/10/1918
War Diary	Couroir	12/10/1918	12/10/1918
War Diary	Avesnes-Lez-Aubert	13/10/1918	13/10/1918
War Diary	Montrecourt	14/10/1918	17/10/1918
War Diary	Proville	18/10/1918	18/10/1918
War Diary	Velu	19/10/1918	21/10/1918
War Diary	Courcelles Lez-Lens	24/10/1918	24/10/1918
War Diary	Frais Marais	26/10/1918	26/10/1918
War Diary	Douai	30/10/1918	30/10/1918
Heading	War Diary Of Y/52nd T.M. Battery From 1st October 1918 To 31st October 1918		
War Diary	Noreuil	01/10/1918	01/10/1918
War Diary	Cantaing	03/10/1918	03/10/1918
War Diary	Moeuvres	05/10/1918	05/10/1918
War Diary	Cantaing	08/10/1918	09/10/1918
War Diary	Niergnies	11/10/1918	11/10/1918
War Diary	Cauroir	12/10/1918	12/10/1918
War Diary	Avesnes-Lez-Aubert	13/10/1918	14/10/1918
War Diary	Montrecourt	15/10/1918	16/10/1918
War Diary	Avesnes-Lez-Aubert	17/10/1918	17/10/1918
War Diary	Cambrai (Faubourg St Sepulchre)	18/10/1918	18/10/1918
War Diary	Lebucquiere	19/10/1918	19/10/1918
War Diary	Velu	21/10/1918	21/10/1918
War Diary	Ecurie	21/10/1918	21/10/1918
War Diary	Courcelles-Lez-Lens	24/10/1918	24/10/1918
War Diary	Frais Marais	26/10/1918	26/10/1918
War Diary	Douai	30/10/1918	30/10/1918
Heading	War Diary Of X/52nd T.M. Bty From 1st November 1918 To 30th November 1918		
War Diary	Douai	01/11/1918	02/11/1918
War Diary	Sameon	06/11/1918	08/11/1918
War Diary	Sirault	15/11/1918	15/11/1918
War Diary	Neufvilles	30/11/1918	30/11/1918
Heading	War Diary Of Y/52nd T.M. Battery From 1st November 1918 To 30th November 1918		
War Diary	Douai	01/11/1918	02/11/1918

War Diary	Sameon	06/11/1918	08/11/1918
War Diary	Sirault	15/11/1918	15/11/1918
War Diary	Neufvilles	30/11/1918	30/11/1918
Heading	War Diary Of "X" 52nd Trench Mortar Battery From 1st December 1918 To 31st December 1918		
War Diary	Neufvilles-En-Gage	01/12/1918	27/12/1918
Heading	War Diary Of "Y" 52nd Trench Mortar Battery From 1st Decr 1918 To 31st Decr. 1918		
War Diary	Neufvilles-En-Gage	01/12/1918	27/12/1918

WO95/2892/4
Divisional Trench Mortar
Batteries

52ND DIVISION

TRENCH MORTAR BTYS.
MAY-DEC 1918

Confidential.

Original

War Diary

of

X.52 Trench Mortar Battery.

from
1.5.18.

to
31.5.18

X/52 T.M. Battery

WAR DIARY or INTELLIGENCE SUMMARY
Army Form C. 2118.
(Erase heading not required.)

Place	Date	Hour	Summary of Events and Information	Remarks and references to Appendices
VALHEUREUX	1st May 1918		At Reserve Army School of Mortars. The old 133, 134, 2nd T.M Batteries combined to form Y/52 T.M.B. New Y/40 T.M.B joined from 40th Division, to become Y/52, completing new 3rd Line T.M. Batteries.	
	1st May to 11th May		Undergoing course at Reserve Army School of Mortars.	
	11th May		Left School & after circuitous train journey arrived on	
NEUVILLE ST VAAST	12th May		at NEUVILLE ST VAAST, joining DTMO 52nd Division & Y/52 T.M.B, who had gone on before. Took over 3 guns in position from Y/52	
VIMY SECTOR	12th May to 14th May		Work was carried out making new emplacements & getting in removing these guns, the whole of the guns being of a defensive character, to fire on S.O.S. 2 more pits were dug in WILLERVAL & guns put in these & 2 pits were dug behind railway embankment in front of FARBUS, and a forward pit was dug [ ] at T.28.d 7.0 for the purpose of offensive action against them T.M. in ARLEUX.	
	end of month		By the end of the month all these guns were in action, and the Battery was prepared to fire all 16 guns on S.O.S. having an average of about 120 rounds complete at each gun. Emplacements to new billets at NEUVILLE ST VAAST were also carried	

Army Form C. 2118.

WAR DIARY
or
INTELLIGENCE SUMMARY.
(Erase heading not required.)

out, the whole of the battery were put through a Mustard Gas Chamber to test Box Respirators. Found satisfactory except 3, which were replaced.

Battery received 6 reinforcements during month, making it at full strength at end of month. Casualties Nil.

Olau Maylu
CAPTAIN.
D.T.M.O. 52ND DIVISION.
for OC X/52 TMB

Original
Not 1.

Consolidated war Diary
of
Y53 French Mortar Bank.

From   To
8 May 1918   31st May 1918

WAR DIARY

INTELLIGENCE SUMMARY

Y52 Trench Mortar Battery, Army Form C. 2118.

May, 1918.

Place	Date	Hour	Summary of Events and Information	Remarks and references to Appendices
VALHEUREUX (near Doullens)	1st	—	At the commencement of the month the battery was at the Reserve Army school of Mortars. It had come from the 40th Division under Army orders, and its title was now changed from Y40 T.M.B. to Y52, as recorded in last month's Diary. The D.T.M.O. 40th Division, accompanied the battery, while another battery from the 52nd Division was also at the school, and became X 52 T.M.B. Thus the 52nd Divisional Trench Mortars were formed. The whole underwent a course of Instruction at the school.	
"	7th	8 p.m.	Sudden orders were received that the battery, together with the D.T.M.O., was to move off at once, two lorries having been sent by the Army for the purpose. All the guns, and as many men as possible, were loaded into these two lorries, and a start was made at 10 p.m.	
MONT ST. ELOY	8th	10 a.m. 3:30 p.m.	In the middle of the night the battery arrived here, in the 52nd Division area. The division was in the XVIII Corps, which had just relieved the Canadian Corps. Accomodation was found for the battery, and everyone turned in for the remainder of the night. The officer Captain from 52nd D.A. arrived, with instructions for the battery to take over the Trench Mortar positions from the 5th Canadian Division and the 15th Division. The Battery Commander went round the line during the day with the Canadian officer, and took over the positions.	
VIMY — ACHEVILLE Road.	"	10 p.m.	The same night half of the battery went into the line with three guns, which	

WAR DIARY
Y52 Trench Mortar Battery
Army Form C. 2118.

INTELLIGENCE SUMMARY
May, 1918 (continued).

Place	Date	Hour	Summary of Events and Information	Remarks and references to Appendices
VIMY-ACHEVILLE Road.	8th	10 p.m.	were moved till one the positions taken over. From the 15th Division three guns were to be taken over complete, and arrangements were made for these to be taken over the following day.	
Left of WILLERVAL	9th	—	A party was detailed to take over the three guns which were now taken over from the 15th Division. These were situated on the road running from WILLERVAL towards AVION. They were manned by the battery until X52 T.M.B. should arrive to take them over.	
VIMY-ACHEVILLE Road.	9th	—	Work was at once commenced on the emplacements to improve them and provide them with cover. Two guns in the MONT FORET QUARRIES required a great deal of work to make their emplacements serviceable. The third gun was behind the Railway Embankment south of VIMY STATION, and was in a fairly good emplacement.	
	12th	—	The three guns in the WILLERVAL sector were handed over to X52 T.M.B., which had at length returned from the School of Mortars.	
	14th	—	A truck was commenced with the purpose of linking up to the track system the quarry in which the two guns were in action. This occupied some six days, the whole battery being employed on it.	
NEUVILLE ST. VAAST.	10th	—	Meanwhile the rear Headquarters of the battery had been moved forward from MONT ST. ELOY to NEUVILLE ST. VAAST, this making communication and all-ifs a real more	

WAR DIARY
INTELLIGENCE SUMMARY

Y.52 Trench Mortar Battery   Army Form C. 2118.

May 1918 (continued).

Place	Date	Hour	Summary of Events and Information	Remarks and references to Appendices
NEUVILLE ST. VAAST.			easy matter. Hence a hut camp was emptied, and all new huts west of the line were employed in improving it. A hut was erected capable of accommodating the whole of the half-battery out of the line; new cook-house and an ablution shed were constructed; and separate quarters made for the N.C.O's.	
VIMY-ACHEVILLE Road.	24th	—	Having completed the improvements to all the existing gunpits, a new one was started in the QUARRY, together with a large ammunition recess which marks to act as a dump when offensive work was commenced in the front line.	
	25th	—	Division required that all guns should be in action by the 28th. One of the new guns to go temporarily into an QUARRY emplacement; one to be taken over complete from X.52 T.M.B., and the 3rd to be put in the existing emplacement, near the front reserve gun. Work was commenced on the above without delay.	
	28th	—	All six guns now in action. One was taken over from X.52 T.M.B., one the WILLERVAL Road, about 500 yards south of MONT FORET QUARRIES; another put to be built was it. Three guns are now in the QUARRY, and two in the railway embankment south of VIMY STATION. Till the end of the month, the battery was fully employed on the completion of all these emplacements.	

Montalegre Link
O.C. Y.52 T.M.B.

Headquarters,
52nd Division.
━━━━━━━━━━━━

A.G./527/17/P.S.

X/52 and
War Diary of ⁁Y/52 Trench Mortar Battery for June 1918, has been received in this office having been wrongly addressed to A.G., G.H.Q. (in an ordinary envelope, and without a covering letter) and has been passed to D.A.G. 3rd Echelon.

Will you please call the attention of the Officer concerned to G.R.O. 1598.

(SD.) J. S. CAMERON,
LT.-COL., A.A.G.,
FOR
Adjutant General.

G.H.Q.,
1st Echelon,
6 July, 1918.

D.A.G.,
3rd Echelon.
━━━━━━━━━━━━

Forwarded.

Secret

G.H.Q.,
1st Echelon,
16 July, 1918.

[signature]
Lieut.-Colonel
for Adjutant General.

X/52.
T.M. BATTERY
R.F.A.

Date June 1918

WAR DIARY

INTELLIGENCE SUMMARY

(Erase heading not required.)

Army Form C. 2118.

Instructions regarding War Diaries and Intelligence Summaries are contained in F. S. Regs., Part II. and the Staff Manual respectively. Title pages will be prepared in manuscript.

Place	Date	Hour	Summary of Events and Information	Remarks and references to Appendices
NEUVILLE ST VAAST	1st		Battery Headquarters remained here during the month. Men not in the line have been employed throughout the month in improving the camp; a new cookhouse, mess room, etc., was built.	
	3rd to 5th	5.40 p.m.	10 Rounds fired from No. 7 Gun.	
			Men in the line were working on No. 7 & No. 8 Gun pits.	
	6th	5.45 /-	10 Rounds were fired from No. 7 Gun	
	7th	5.30 p.m.	10 Rounds area fire from No. 7 Gun	
WILLERVAL	8th to 13th		All men in the line were working on the Willerval Guns and pits	
	14th	5.40 p.m.	47 Rounds were fired from No. 7 Gun.	
	15th to 18th		Men worked and completed No. 7 & 8 Gun Emplacements.	
	19th	5.20 p.m.	20 Rounds fired from No. 7 Gun.	
	20th	5.25 p.m.	24 Rounds fired from No. 7 Gun. Men employed in generally improving gun emplacements.	
	23rd	5.40 p.m.	21 Rounds fired from No. 8 Gun. Men engaged clearing Guns & bombs.	
	25th		6 Rounds fired from No. 7 Gun and 6 from No. 8 Gun. This a manoeuvre of Fahrer,	
			Reg. Standard & some Concrete were added also for new positions.	
	27th	5.30 p.m.	Fire 30 rounds from No. 7 + 10 from No. 8 Guns. One man was killed + one wounded near emerald while conveying ammo to Battery at night	

Army Form C. 2118.

X/52.
T.M. BATTERY
R.F.A.
Date June 1918.

WAR DIARY
or
INTELLIGENCE SUMMARY.
(Erase heading not required.)

Instructions regarding War Diaries and Intelligence Summaries are contained in F. S. Regs., Part II. and the Staff Manual respectively. Title pages will be prepared in manuscript.

Place	Date	Hour	Summary of Events and Information	Remarks and references to Appendices
FARBUS Sta.	28th	5.40 p.m.	Fired 16 rounds from No. 8 gun. There were four men sick with influenza.	
	29th		Commenced digging new positions at Fabus the Rly. Embankment & Lone Tree, this work was continued on the 30th.	
	30th	5.30 p.m.	Fired 20 rounds from No. 8 Gun.	

A. M. Munro Capt. RFA.
Comdg. X/52. T.M.B. RFA.

Army Form C. 2118.

WAR DIARY
INTELLIGENCE SUMMARY.
(Erase heading not required.)

V/52 TRENCH MORTAR BATTERY.

June, 1918.

Place	Date	Hour	Summary of Events and Information	Remarks and references to Appendices
NEUVILLE ST. VAAST.	1st	—	Battery Headquarters remained here during the month. Men who were out of the line were employed on the improvement of the camp; and new huts, cookhouse, wash rooms, etc., were built.	
VIMY—ACHEVILLE road.	1st	—	Advanced Headquarters were on the road, while the guns were ditched in depth along the road. Two were mounted behind the railway embankment to the right of VIMY STATION, and three were in MONT FORÊT QUARRIES.	
	4th	9 pm	Work was commenced on a forward emplacement nearly 1000 yards forward from MONT FORÊT QUARRIES, placed so as to cover the village of ACHEVILLE. This work had to be carried out by night.	
MONT FORÊT— WILLERVAL road.	4th	—	The sector of the Battery was extended to the right, and work was also in progress on two gun pits on this road near the west of the hill.	
MONT FORÊT QUARRIES	8th 9th	3 am	The position here was badly shelled with Yellow Cross Gas, and as a consequence the enemy was avoided all parts of the day.	
MONT FORÊT— ARLEUX road.	13th	—	Another forward position was selected on the right of this road to cover the work of ARLEUX village. Work was commenced on this immediately.	
MONT FORÊT— ACHEVILLE road.	15th	—	The forward emplacement here, which was commenced on the 4th, was now completed.	
	17th	—	An epidemic of influenza broke out in the Battery and latest to the end of the month. So many men reported sick that it was only with the utmost difficulty that the work could be carried on.	

Army Form C. 2118.

Y/52
TRENCH MORTAR
BATTERY.

June, 1918 (contd.)

WAR DIARY
—
INTELLIGENCE SUMMARY.
(Erase heading not required.)

Instructions regarding War Diaries and Intelligence Summaries are contained in F. S. Regs., Part II. and the Staff Manual respectively. Title pages will be prepared in manuscript.

Place	Date	Hour	Summary of Events and Information	Remarks and references to Appendices
MONT FORÊT — WILLERVAL and VIMY	21st	—	Positions in this sector completed.	
	29th	—	Owing to change of disposition in the XVIII Corps, orders were received to withdraw the guns behind the LENS–ARRAS railway. A reconnaissance of VIMY and the ground north of it was made, and sites were selected for our section under the railway embankment near BOIS DE LA CHAUDIÈRE, and for another section in the N.E. edge of VIMY village. The third section was to remain in its old site on the right of VIMY STATION. One gun was to remain forward in MONT FORÊT QUARRIES for offensive purposes.	
BOIS DE LA CHAUDIÈRE	28th	—	Work was commenced on the positions for this section, and continued to the end of the month.	

Marshall Capt.
O.C. Y/52.T.M.B.

WAR DIARY

52nd DIVISIONAL ARTILLERY TRENCH MORTARS.

JULY 1st 1918.   to   July 31st 1918.

Volume 1   Part VII

WAR DIARY of X/52. T.M. Battery R.F.A. Army Form C. 2118.

INTELLIGENCE SUMMARY. for the month of July 1918

(Erase heading not required.)

Instructions regarding War Diaries and Intelligence Summaries are contained in F. S. Regs., Part II. and the Staff Manual respectively. Title pages will be prepared in manuscript.

Place	Date	Hour	Summary of Events and Information	Remarks and references to Appendices
NEUVILLE ST. VAAST	1918 1st July		Guns in action between MILLERIM & MERICOURT. Head Quarters of Battery still here. The men out of the line were employed to finish building new cook-house, white-washing the interior, putting up shelves and making new meat safe. Men in the line were digging new gun pits. Fired 30 rounds.	
	3rd		Men in line still employed digging gun pits and cleaning Ammunition. Fired 20 rounds.	
	4		Men out of the line were busy banking up and sandbagging round new Messing Hut.	
	5		Men in the line still employed digging and cleaning ammunition. Fired 30 rounds.	
	6		Fired 18 rounds.	
	7		Men out of line were kept busy re-banking the Messing round Billets	

WAR DIARY of X/52.T.M.Battery R.F.A.

Army Form C. 2118.

INTELLIGENCE SUMMARY.

for the month of July '18 (Cont)

(Erase heading not required.)

Place	Date	Hour	Summary of Events and Information	Remarks and references to Appendices
	1918 July 7 (cont)		which was cooled down by the heavy storms	
	8th		At about 6.0. A.M. the forward cookhouse was shot away and some of the mens equipment destroyed by enemy bombardment which lasted approximately half an hour and consisted of 4.2 and 6.9 shells.	
	9h		Men in Lines still employed digging gun pits. Enemy Aeroplane brought down.	
	10h		Men at Hdqrs. Quarters employed making new roof and floor in Bty. Office. 22 round retired enemy retaliated but no advance no casualties	
	11h		Bulls temporary forward cookhouse.	
	13h		Still digging gun pits and Ammunition recesses. Prospects of new forward Hdqrs Quarters destroyed.	
	15h		Men out of the line busy digging drainage trenches round Messing Hut.	
	16h		Gun pit by Sunk Tree finished X.1. X.3. X.4. and Willerval pits. Ammunition at Willerval and Zouzval handed over to Canadians together with two guns complete	

WAR DIARY of X/52 T.M. Battery R.F.A. for the month of July '18. (Cont.)

INTELLIGENCE SUMMARY

Army Form C. 2118.

(Erase heading not required.)

Place	Date	Hour	Summary of Events and Information	Remarks and references to Appendices
	1918 July 17th		Men on the line employed improving gun pits and clearing ammunition	
	18th		X6 and Y11 Lines altered. Took over two guns, pits and ammunition from Y Bty.	
in Ottawa				
	19th		Men in lines still busy digging and improving pits already dug.	
			Took two guns back from Cambrai	
	20th		Men and of the Bre employed generally improving the camp.	
			Enemy Aeroplane brought down	
	21st		Relieved by 8th Divisional Artillery. One Officer admitted to Hospital	
	22nd		On the move, proceeded to OURTON in transport, and took over guns etc. left	
			behind by 8th Divl. Artillery. Battery stayed here until 29th inst., weather during two	
			stops was very wet.	

WAR DIARY of X/52 T.M. Battery R.F.A.

for the month of July 15 (Cont)

Army Form C. 2118.

(Erase heading not required.)

Place	Date	Hour	Summary of Events and Information	Remarks and references to Appendices
	1915 July			
	29		Moved to Matagascar Camp to relieve 5th Canadians	
	30		Took over guns, ammunition and pits from St Canadians	
	31		Moved Battery Head Quarters to Anzin	

Adam Minor
Capt. R.F.A.
Comdg X/52 T.M. Batty R.F.A.

Army Form C. 2118.

WAR DIARY
or
INTELLIGENCE SUMMARY
(Erase heading not required.)

Y/52 TRENCH MORTAR BATTERY.

July, 1918.

Place	Date	Hour	Summary of Events and Information	Remarks and references to Appendices
NEUVILLE ST. VAAST. VIMY	1st	—	Headquarters of the Battery at Neuville St. Vaast.	
VIMY	1st	—	Advanced Headquarters at Vimy, on the northern edge of the village. One section of guns in action to cover the main line of defence, behind the railway embankment on the right of Vimy Station. Another section behind Railway Embankment on the right of La Maudire Wood.	
VIMY–ACHEVILLE ROAD	2nd	12 noon	Advanced gun 1,000 yards in front of Mont St. Quentin fired on uncompleted trench works in Acheville. Meanwhile work was energetically continued on the completion of the gun pits of the two reserve sections intended about work in position for the third section; its new	
VIMY	10th	8 pm	Advanced Hqrs. north of VIMY.	
	14th	—	The first two sections were now completed, and all work was concentrated on the third section, commenced on the 10th.	
	21st	—	Sector handed over with all guns and ammunition to Y8 Trench Mortar Battery. Personnel brought down to Hqrs. at Neuville St. Vaast.	
NEUVILLE ST. VAAST. OURTON	22nd 22nd	10 am —	Battery moved in lorries to Ourton. Battery camped here in G.H.Q. reserve.	

Army Form C. 2118.

Y/52
TRENCH MORTAR BATTERY.

No. ....
Date July 19.18 (opt. round).

WAR DIARY
INTELLIGENCE SUMMARY.
(Erase heading not required.)

Instructions regarding War Diaries and Intelligence Summaries are contained in F. S. Regs., Part II. and the Staff Manual respectively. Title pages will be prepared in manuscript.

Place	Date	Hour	Summary of Events and Information	Remarks and references to Appendices
OURTON	29th	—	Battery moved from Ourton to Maizieres Camp in Arras-Bethune Roads, preparatory to taking over positions in the line.	
BAILLEUL	30th	—	Positions taken over from 54th Canadian Div. Trench Mortars. One 9.45" Trench Mortar, and one 6" T.M. in active positions on the right of the Arras-Gavrelle Road; eight 6" Trench Mortars in defensive positions to the right of Bailleul; and Advanced Headquarters in the Railway Cutting to the right of Bailleul Station.	
ANZIN	31st	—	Rear Headquarters moved to Anzin; taking over the 5th C.D.T.M. Camp. Total Casualties—5; Total Reinforcements—10; Total rounds fired 7123.	

Blackmore
....................CAPTAIN,
O.C. Y52 TRENCH MORTAR BATTERY.

CONFIDENTIAL.

ORIGINAL.

WAR DIARY

O F

X/52 TRENCH MORTAR BATTERY.

FROM – 1st AUGUST 1918.   TO – 31st AUGUST 1918.

Army Form C. 2118.

X/52 TRENCH MORTAR BATTERY, R.F.A.

No. ....
Date August 1918.

WAR DIARY
or
INTELLIGENCE SUMMARY.
(Erase heading not required.)

Instructions regarding War Diaries and Intelligence Summaries are contained in F. S. Regs., Part II. and the Staff Manual respectively. Title pages will be prepared in manuscript.

Place	Date	Hour	Summary of Events and Information	Remarks and references to Appendices
ANZIN ST. AUBIN	1st		Headquarters were situated here throughout the month.	
11TH OF SCARPE			Battery relieved by part of X/57 Trench Mortar Battery, one officer left in this position to hand over. Remainder came out and arrived at ANZIN 10.30 p.m.	
WILLERVAL	2nd		Trench Battery positions taken over from 4th Canadian Trench Mortar Battery.	
11TH OF SCARPE			Relief completed with X/57 Trench Mortar Battery.	
WILLERVAL	4th		Fired 17 rounds from No.7 forward gun.	
	5th		Fired 12 rounds from No.7 forward guns, and 19 rounds from No.8 forward gun.	
	6th		Commenced work on new positions in accordance with fresh plan.	
	7th		The Hun made a raid in front of WILLERVAL about 12.15 midnight. 16 rounds fired on Enemy Earthworks East of.	
	8th		Men working on new positions.	
			WILLERVAL from No.8 forward gun.	
	9th	12.45 a.m.	Good progress now made in new positions. Two of these guns ready for action.	
			Projector Gas 2nd over from in front of WILLERVAL, no retaliation. No.5 gun ready for action.	
	10th		Battery still employed making new positions. Two more completed and ready for action.	

Army Form C. 2118.

X/52
TRENCH MORTAR
BATTERY. R.F.A.
No ....
Date Aug 1918.

WAR DIARY
or
INTELLIGENCE SUMMARY
(Erase heading not required.)

Instructions regarding War Diaries and Intelligence Summaries are contained in F. S. Regs., Part II. and the Staff Manual respectively. Title pages will be prepared in manuscript.

Summary of Events and Information

Place	Date	Hour	Summary of Events and Information	Remarks and references to Appendices
WILLERVAL	11th		Turned out in response to A.O.S. at about 3 o'c. a.m., and set up in four places on Right and one on Left. Boche Shots with Minnies and 3 or 4 - 5.9's.	
	14th		Men still working on new positions. Two guns in reserve positions behind WILLERVAL. Two guns in reserve positions behind LENS - ARRAS RAILWAY, in front of FARBUS STATION. Two guns in sunken road between BAILLEUL and Sugar Factory.	
	22nd		Battery withdrawn and positions handed over to Y/8 Trench Mortar Battery.	
ANZIN ST. AUBIN			Owing to orders to move being cancelled the Battery remained here at rest until the end of the month. Two other Ranks admitted to hospital during the month.	

M Arthur
Capt. R.F.A.
Comdg. X/52 Trench Mortar Battery R.F.A.

CONFIDENTIAL.   ORIGINAL.

WAR DIARY

OF

Y/52 TRENCH MORTAR BATTERY.

FROM - 1st AUGUST 1918.

31st AUGUST 1918.

WAR DIARY
INTELLIGENCE SUMMARY.
(Erase heading not required)

Army Form C. 2118.

Y/52 TRENCH MORTAR BATTERY.

August, 1918.

Place	Date	Hour	Summary of Events and Information	Remarks and references to Appendices
ANZIN ST. AUBIN. BAILLEUL	1st	—	Rear Headquarters were situated here throughout the month.	
	1st	—	Advanced Headquarters was in the railway cutting south of Bailleul Station; one gun was in action to the north of the station; no rear Headquarters; two in sunken road south of the village; and one in an advanced position on the right of the Arras–Gavrelle road. Firing was carried out with this gun until the 6th on enemy trenches south-west of Gavrelle. There were also four guns in reserve positions in front of the Bois de la Maison Blanche.	
	6th	—	Advanced guns on right of Gavrelle Road withdrawn to Headquarters. A reconnaissance was made with a view to the adoption of a new scheme for forward guns in the front system east of Bailleul, and six defensive pits on the line of the Arras–Lens railway.	
	8th	—	Work commenced on above outlined above. One no. 6H near Headquarters, and one to the north of the station commenced.	
	13th	—	Both new guns in action. Battery was distributed in this action — one in sunken road south of Bailleul; one near Headquarters; one north of station. These are guns to cover the main line of defence (Battzeel).	

Army Form C. 2118.

WAR DIARY
INTELLIGENCE SUMMARY.
(Erase heading not required.)

V/52 TRENCH MORTAR BATTERY.

August, 1918 (continued).

Place	Date	Hour	Summary of Events and Information	Remarks and references to Appendices
BAILLEUL	17th	—	All guns taken out of action and preparations made for operations on Bank of River Scarpe.	
River SCARPE W. of FAMPOUX	17th	—	Work carried out to get guns in action here, to fire across the river in support of operations on south bank. Operations cancelled in the evening.	
BAILLEUL	18th	—	Guns re-mounted, and normal conditions resumed.	
	20th	—	Left section withdrawn, and positions handed over to Y8 Trench Mortar Battery. Remaining section also withdrawn, and positions handed over to 6×6" Trench Mortar Battery.	
ANZIN ST. AUBIN.	21st	—	Orders to move having been cancelled, the Battery remained here awaiting orders.	
	23rd	8 p.m.	Orders received to carry out operation on the Scarpe as on 17th. Guns and beds sent up.	
River SCARPE W. of FAMPOUX.	24th	—	Guns placed in action in a drained trench on south side of Arras–Gavrelle Road. Ammunition brought up by wagon at night.	
	25th	—	Ammunition dumped and final preparations made. The Battery was to fire on the eastern end of the railway cutting of the Arras–Douai railway on the

Army Form C. 2118.

Y/52 TRENCH MORTAR BATTERY.

WAR DIARY

INTELLIGENCE SUMMARY
(Erase heading not required.)

August, 1918 (contd.)

Instructions regarding War Diaries and Intelligence Summaries are contained in F. S. Regs., Part II. and the Staff Manual respectively. Title pages will be prepared in manuscript.

Place	Date	Hour	Summary of Events and Information	Remarks and references to Appendices
River SCARPE W. of FAMPOUX	26th	3 a.m.	west bank of the river. Ranging round fired. Zero hour. Fire was opened, every gun firing gunfire. Four 77 mm shells were fired in retaliation, but started from one of these damaged one of the guns so as to put it out of action. The remaining guns each fired 100 rounds. Fire ceased at 3.30 am.	
	27/.	—	During the day the guns were taken out of action. Owing to the advance of the Canadian Corps and capture of MONCHY, it was possible to withdraw the guns in daylight by men. The Battery remained in rest here until the end of the month.	
ANZIN ST. AUBIN	27/.	—		

Total Casualties — nil. Reinforcements — 3. Strength on 31st — 58.

.... CAPTAIN,
O.C. Y62 TRENCH MORTAR BATTERY.

Original

Vol 5

Confidential

War Diary of 4/152. I.N. Batty.

From 1st Sept 1918.
To 30 Sept 1918

Army Form C. 2118.

WAR DIARY
or
INTELLIGENCE SUMMARY.

(Erase heading not required.)

Y/52 TRENCH MORTAR BATTERY.

SEPTEMBER 1918.

Instructions regarding War Diaries and Intelligence Summaries are contained in F. S. Regs., Part II. and the Staff Manual respectively. Title pages will be prepared in manuscript.

Place	Date	Hour	Summary of Events and Information	Remarks and references to Appendices
ANZIN-ST-AUBIN	1-9-18		Battery was in rest at Anzin until the 11th inst.	
CROISILLES	11-9-18		Battery rejoined Division at Croisilles, and remained until the 14th inst.	
QUEANT	14-9-18		Battery moved up to Queant. Battery had orders to get 6 guns in action in Moeuvres on the night of the 14th. On the night of the 14th the enemy successfully attacked and retook Moeuvres, this of course making it impossible for the guns to be put in.	
QUEANT	16-9-18		Battery suffered casualties:- 2 killed and 5 wounded. Battery had orders to place 2 guns in action on the Hindenburg Line, about 100 yards N.W. of Moeuvres. This was found to be impossible owing to the enemy being within 30 yards of that position.	
QUEANT	19-9-18		Enemy was forced to evacuate Moeuvres.	

Confidential.

Original

War Diary of X./152 I. M. Boats

From:-
1st Sept. 1918

To:-
30 Sept. 1918

Army Form C. 2118.

X/52 TRENCH MORTAR BATTERY. R.F.A.
Sept 1918

WAR DIARY
INTELLIGENCE SUMMARY.
(Erase heading not required.)

Instructions regarding War Diaries and Intelligence Summaries are contained in F. S. Regs., Part II. and the Staff Manual respectively. Title pages will be prepared in manuscript.

Place	Date	Hour	Summary of Events and Information	Remarks and references to Appendices
ANZIN ST. AUBIN.	1-9-18		The Battery remained here at rest, until the 11th inst.	
CROISILLES	11-9-18		Reported Division at Croisilles on the 11th inst, and Battery were employed on Salvage work, until the 15th inst.	
MOEUVRES	16-9-18		Battery went into line, and took over two forward Guns in outskirts of MOEUVRES, from X/57 T.M.Bty. on the 16th inst.	
	17-9-18		Enemy Attack MOEUVRES, two forward Guns destroyed by Shell fire. Detachments withdrawn to forward Headquarters in Hindenburg Line.	
	18-9-18		Battery sustained the following Casualties. 3 killed and 31 wounded. Shell Gas a Smoke. Battery Amalgamated X and Y Batteries to form one Battery, owing to Hospital. Shortage of Personnel.	
	19-9-18		Enemy driven out of MOEUVRES, by counter attack.	
	20-9-18		Guns put in on North West outskirts of MOEUVRES, and commenced firing on the wire, East of the Canal de Nord, opposite MOEUVRES.	
	21/22/23-9-18		Continued firing on the wire, & taking Western Necessary.	
	24-9-18		Received orders to put two Guns in position along with the Bty. to co-operate in the first phase of the operations. Guns taken up to dip same night.	

Army Form C. 2118.

X/52 TRENCH MORTAR BATTERY, R.F.A.

No. ....
Date. Sept. 1918.

WAR DIARY
INTELLIGENCE SUMMARY.
(Erase heading not required.)

Instructions regarding War Diaries and Intelligence Summaries are contained in F. S. Regs., Part II. and the Staff Manual respectively. Title pages will be prepared in manuscript.

Place	Date	Hour	Summary of Events and Information	Remarks and references to Appendices
MOEUVRES	24-9-18		MOEUVRES Guns continued to fire on the wire.	
	25-9-18		MOEUVRES Guns completed firing on the wire. Sample dug and Guns got into action at the Sky. Ammunition taken up to these positions	
	26-9-18		Continued work on Guns at the Sky	
	29-9-18		General attack. - Guns fired 75 rounds each on the Canal du Nord.	
	25/30-9-18		Removed Guns from old positions. Battery with XVII to QUEANT	
			TOTAL CASUALTIES. - 3 killed in Action. 31 Wounded Shell Gas.	
			2. Admitted to Hospital Sick	
			8. O.R. arks posted from 52nd DAC.	
			12. O.R.anks " " R.H.&R.F.A. DETAILS - BASE.	

W M Murray
Capt. RFA.
Comdg. X/52 T.M.Bty., RFA.

ORIGINAL.

WAR DIARY OF X/52nd T.M. BATTERY.

CONFIDENTIAL.

FROM - 1st OCTOBER 1918   TO - 31st OCTOBER 1918.

Army Form C. 2118.

WAR DIARY
or
INTELLIGENCE SUMMARY.
(Erase heading not required.)

X/52 TRENCH MORTAR BATTERY, R.F.A.

Date October 1918.

Place	Date	Hour	Summary of Events and Information	Remarks and references to Appendices
NOREUIL	1st		Battery lying here in reserve, having been withdrawn after the fight at MOEUVRES	
	3rd		Moved from NOREUIL to D.A.C., near CANTAING.	
CANTAING	4th		Moved into village. One man wounded	
MOEUVRES	5th		Owing to uncertain conditions Battery moved frequently.	
CANTAING	8/10th		Enemy aircraft bombed this camp.	
NIERGNIES	11th		The Battery now followed up the advance, after the capture of CAMBRAI	
COUROIR AVESNES-LEZ-AUBERT	12th 13th		Battery Head Quarters established here.	
MONTRÉCOURT	14th		Received orders to get one mobile gun into position in the neighbourhood of MONTRÉCOURT, to cover junction of road and railway on the East of the river SELLE.	
	16th		Took part in attack on river SELLE.	
	16th		Mobile guns in action at MONTRÉCOURT	
	17th		Guns withdrawn	
PROVILLE	18th		Battery marched here with Divisional Artillery	
VELU	19th		Moved again with Divisional Artillery	
	21st		Battery entrained here for transfer to the First Army, and arrived at MADAGASCAR Camp same day	

Army Form C. 2118.

X/52
TRENCH MORTAR
BATTERY, R.F.A.

Name ....
Date October 1918

WAR DIARY

~~INTELLIGENCE SUMMARY~~

(Erase heading not required.)

Place	Date	Hour	Summary of Events and Information	Remarks and references to Appendices
COURCELLES LEZ - LENS	24th		Battery marched forward to rejoin Division	
FRAIS MARAIS	26th			
DOUAI	30th		Attached to Divisional Reception Camp at DOUAI to await arrival of Guns and Stores from dump at ACHIET - LE - GRAND.	
			CASUALTIES — 1 O.R. wounded.	
			ADMITTED TO HOSPITAL SICK } 3 O.Rs.	
			& STRUCK OFF STRENGTH	
			TRANSFERS 9 O.Rs. to 9th BDE., R.F.A.	
			EFFECTIVE STRENGTH 3 OFFICERS 444 O RANKS.	

[signature]
Capt., R.F.A.
Comdg X/52 T.M.By., R.F.A.

CONFIDENTIAL.

ORIGINAL.

Vol 6

WAR DIARY OF Y/52nd T. M. BATTERY.

* * * * * * * * * * * * * * *

FROM 1st OCTOBER 1918   TO 31st OCTOBER 1918.

Army Form C. 2118.

WAR DIARY
or
INTELLIGENCE SUMMARY.
(Erase heading not required.)

Y/52 TRENCH MORTAR BATTERY.

OCTOBER. 1918.

Instructions regarding War Diaries and Intelligence Summaries are contained in F. S. Regs. Part II. and the Staff Manual respectively. Title pages will be prepared in manuscript.

Place	Date	Hour	Summary of Events and Information	Remarks and references to Appendices
NOREUIL.	1ST.	-	Battery was in reserve here, having been withdrawn after the fight at MOEUVRES. Owing to the uncertain conditions the Battery moved frequently.	
CANTAING.	3RD.	-		
MOEUVRES.	5TH.			
CANTAING.	8TH.			
"	9TH.		Camp was bombed by enemy aircraft. One officer was wounded.	
NIERGNIES.	11TH.		The Battery now followed up the advance after the capture of CAMBRAI.	
CAUROIR.	12TH.			
AVESNES-LEZ-AUBERT.	13TH.			
"	14TH.		Battery Head Quarters was established here. Orders were received to occupy a position with the mobile gun, in the neighbourhood of MONTRÉCOURT, to cover the junction of road and railway on the East of the river SELLE. This gun was put in position in rear of MONTRÉCOURT under cover of darkness.	
MONTRÉCOURT.	15TH.		Ammunition was taken up and final preparations made for bombardment the next morning.	
"	16TH.	0610.	The target given above was bombarded prior to the capture of HAUSSY. During the day and the following night, the Battery stood by in case of a counter attack.	

Army Form C. 2118.

WAR DIARY
or
INTELLIGENCE SUMMARY.

Y/52 TRENCH MORTAR BATTERY.

October 1918.

Place	Date	Hour	Summary of Events and Information	Remarks and references to Appendices
AVESNES-LEZ-AUBERT.	17th.		Mobile gun was brought out of action. Surplus ammunition being taken over by 61st. Divl. Trench Mortars.	
CAMBRAI. (FAUBOURG. ST. SEPULCHRE.)	18th.		Battery withdrawn with the Divisional Artillery, stopping here one night.	
LEBUCQUIERE	19th.		The second days march brought the Battery here for entrainment.	
VELU.	21st.	0015.	Battery entrained for transfer to the First Army.	
ECURIE. COURCELLES-LEZ-LENS.	21st.	9000.	Battery arrived and encamped.	
FRAIS MARAIS.	24th.		Battery marched forward to rejoin the Division.	
DOUAI.	26th.		Attached to Divisional Reception Camp at DOUAI, to await arrival of Guns and stores from dumps at ACHIET-LE-GRAND.	

CASUALTIES :- 1. OFFICER WOUNDED.

ADMITTED TO HOSPITAL SICK } 2. OTHER RANKS.
STRUCK OFF STRENGTH. }

TRANSFERS :- 4. O.Rs. TO 56th BRIGADE. R.F.A.
" 2. O.Rs. TO 9th " "

EFFECTIVE STRENGTH :- OFFICERS - 4. O.RANKS. 52.

.... CAPTAIN,
O.C. Y52 TRENCH MORTAR BATTERY.

Original
987

Confidential

War Diary of X/52nd T.M. Bty.

From
1st November 1918
to
30th November 1918.

Army Form C. 2118.

X/52 TRENCH MORTAR BATTERY, R.F.A.
No. ....
Date November 1918.

WAR DIARY
or
INTELLIGENCE SUMMARY.
(Erase heading not required.)

Instructions regarding War Diaries and Intelligence Summaries are contained in F. S. Regs., Part II. and the Staff Manual respectively. Title pages will be prepared in manuscript.

Place	Date	Hour	Summary of Events and Information	Remarks and references to Appendices
	1918			
DOUAI	Nov. 1st		Battery rested here, pending arrival of Guns & stores dumped in Third Army Area.	
	2nd		Battery was equipped with two mobile carriages, complete, with the new design of bed, with spades. During subsequent days, drill with the new carriages was practised.	
SAMEON	6th		Battery was moved forward, by order of Divisional Commander, in order to test the mobile Guns.	
	7th		A range was selected and preliminary trials carried out. The new Guns were found to be extremely accurate and reliable.	
	8th		Owing to the retirement of the enemy the demonstration arranged could not take place. The Division moved forward but the Trench Mortar Batteries remained at SAMEON.	
SIRAULT	15th		Hostilities having ceased the Battery moved forward to rejoin the Division which was then resting in this area.	
NEUFVILLES	30th		Owing to a change in the Divisional boundary the Battery had to move. The health of the battery during month, was excellent.	

[signature] Capt RFA
Comdg X/52 T.M. Battery, RFA.

Confidential

Original

War Diary
of
Y/ 52nd T.M. Battery

From   To
1st November 1918   30th November 1918

Army Form C. 2118.

V/52
TRENCH MORTAR
BATTERY.

WAR DIARY
or
INTELLIGENCE SUMMARY.
(Erase heading not required.)

NOVEMBER. 1918.

Instructions regarding War Diaries and Intelligence Summaries are contained in F.S. Regs., Part II. and the Staff Manual respectively. Title pages will be prepared in manuscript.

Place	Date	Hour	Summary of Events and Information	Remarks and references to Appendices
DOUAI.	1ST.	—	Battery was resting here pending arrival of Guns and stores dumped in Third Army Area.	
DOUAI.	2ND	—	Battery was equipped with 2 mobile carriages, complete with the new design of Held with shades. During subsequent days, drill with the new carriages was carried out.	
SAMEON.	6TH.	—	Battery was moved forward by order of Divisional Commander, in order to test the mobile Guns.	
SAMEON	7TH	—	A range was selected and preliminary trials carried out. The new guns were found to be extremely accurate and reliable.	
SAMEON.	8TH.	—	Owing to the retirement of the enemy, the demonstration arranged could not take place. The Division moved forward, but the Trench Mortar Batteries remained at SAMEON.	
SIRAULT.	15TH	—	Hostilities having ceased, the Battery moved forward to rejoin the Division, which was then resting in this area.	
NEUFVILLES	30TH	—	Owing to a change in the Divisional boundary the Battery had to move. The rest was continued in the new area.	

Army Form C. 2118.

WAR DIARY
or
~~INTELLIGENCE SUMMARY~~

Y/52 TRENCH MORTAR BATTERY.

NOVEMBER 1918.

(Erase heading not required.)

Instructions regarding War Diaries and Intelligence Summaries are contained in F. S. Regs., Part II. and the Staff Manual respectively. Title pages will be prepared in manuscript.

Place	Date	Hour	Summary of Events and Information	Remarks and references to Appendices
			1. OFFICER transferred to England, sick. — Struck off strength.	
			2. O. RANKS admitted to Hospital. " " "	
			1. O. RANK Rejoined unit from Hospital. — "	

[signature]
.... CAPTAIN,
O.C. Y52 TRENCH MORTAR BATTERY.

Confidential.

Original
T.B.8

War Diary of

"X" 52nd Trench Mortar Battery

from 1st December 1918.
to 31st December 1918

Army Form C. 2118.

WAR DIARY

~~INTELLIGENCE~~ SUMMARY

(Erase heading not required.)

X/52 TRENCH MORTAR BATTERY, R.F.A.

December 1918

Instructions regarding War Diaries and Intelligence Summaries are contained in F. S. Regs., Part II. and the Staff Manual respectively. Title pages will be prepared in manuscript.

Place	Date	Hour	Summary of Events and Information	Remarks and references to Appendices
NEUFVILLES EN-GAGE.	1st		The Battery H.Q. remained here throughout the month. Personnel attached to 52nd D.A.C. were withdrawn.	
	27th		All Trench Mortar personnel with the exception of sufficient men to take care of Guns and Stores, were attached to the batteries of the 56th Brigade R.F.A. Detail work connected with all Trench Mortar personnel is being carried out from these Head Quarters.	
			CASUALTIES	
			1 O.R. admitted to Hospital	
			1 O.R. posted from Base.	

Ninthofpm Capt.
for O.C. X/52 T.M. Bty., R.F.A.

Confidential

Original

from Scout of
"Y" Trench Mortar Battery

From
1st Dec. 1918.

To
31st Dec. 1918.

Army Form C. 2118.

WAR DIARY
or
~~INTELLIGENCE SUMMARY~~
(Erase heading not required.)

V/52 TRENCH MORTAR BATTERY.

DECEMBER 1918.

Instructions regarding War Diaries and Intelligence Summaries are contained in F.S. Regs., Part II. and the Staff Manual respectively. Title pages will be prepared in manuscript.

Place	Date	Hour	Summary of Events and Information	Remarks and references to Appendices
NEUFVILLES-EN-GAGE.	1ST.	—	The Battery H.Q. remained here throughout the whole of the month.	
"	24TH	—	Personnel attached to 52ND. D.A.C. were withdrawn. All Trench Mortar Personnel, with the exception of sufficient men to take care of guns and stores were attached to the batteries of the 56th Brigade. R.F.A. Detail work in connection with all Trench Mortar personnel is being carried out from these H.Q. RE-INFORCEMENTS :- POSTED FROM BASE. 6. O.Rs. STRENGTH. DECREASE :- " TO 9TH. BRIGADE. 1. O.R. " " TO ENGLAND. AS. MINER. 1. O.R. " " FOR DUTY AT } 1. OFFICER. MINISTRY OF LABOUR.	

O. M. .... CAPTAIN,
for. O.C. V52 TRENCH MORTAR BATTERY.

www.ingramcontent.com/pod-product-compliance
Lightning Source LLC
Chambersburg PA
CBHW081455160426
43193CB00013B/2485